PRAYER AND CONTEMPLATION

PRAYER AND CONTEMPLATION

ROBERT LLEWELYN

SLG PRESS
Convent of the Incarnation
Fairacres Oxford
OX4 1TB

Revised Edition 1980

ISBN 0 7283 0085 0
ISSN 0307-1405

CONTENTS

ACKNOWLEDGEMENT

The picture on the cover is 'Road to the North' by Nora S. Unwin, taken from *SHALL WE JOIN THE LADIES? Wood Engravings by Women Artists of the Twentieth Century*, published in 1979 by Betty Clark, Studio One Gallery, Oxford, in a limited edition of 500 at £30.

We wish to express our gratitude to Miss Unwin for so readily granting us permission to use her engraving, and also to Mrs Betty Clark who, with equal readiness, permitted us to bear off a copy of her valuable book for the purpose of making a plate.

PREFACE

Mystical experience is given to some. But contemplation is for all Christians. Allow me to say a word about that prayer which is needed for all of us . . . [It] means essentially our being with God, putting ourselves in his presence, being hungry and thirsty for him, wanting him, letting heart and mind and will move towards him; with the needs of the world on our heart. It is a rhythmic movement of the personality into the eternity and peace of God, and no less for the turmoil of the world for whose sake, as for ours, we are seeking God. If that is the heart of prayer then the contemplative part of it will be large. And a church which starves itself and its members in the contemplative life deserves whatever spiritual leanness it may experience.

This passage from Bishop Michael Ramsey's *Canterbury Pilgrim*, (1974, pp. 59-60) conveys very well the general sense in which the word 'contemplation' is used in this book. In that sense it is, I believe, an experience into which every committed Christian may at some stage expect to be drawn. A growing number of people today are looking to the Churches—and often beyond—to lead them to a new dimension in prayer. These pages are written in the conviction that the key to their search lies within the great tradition of Christian spirituality, and in the hope that many will find in them the encouragement and guidance which they seek.

ROBERT LLEWELYN

CHAPTER 1

Prayer as Petition

I PROPOSE to approach our subject from the angle of *supplication*, a word which describes prayer in all its petitionary and intercessory aspects. Supplication is basic to the very idea of prayer—the etymology of the word *prayer* alone suggests that—and it is, I believe, the way most of us come to prayer, and an indispensable form of it in one way or another throughout our lives.

When the disciples asked Jesus to teach them how to pray he gave them as their model a prayer which is petitionary in form from beginning to end. It is true that it is placed in the setting of adoration, as all supplication to God should be—the first request is that God's name be kept holy. And it is true that the petition is never for selfish personal ends—the corporate aspect of the prayer is safeguarded throughout by the first two words, 'Our Father', reminding us that we make our petition as members of a family, regarding the needs of others with as much concern as our own. It is true, further, that our Lord's prayer lifts our sights far beyond our own small concerns, whether individual or corporate, beyond the horizons of family or community or parish or church or even nation. 'Thy kingdom come', we pray, 'thy will be done, as in heaven so on earth', thus projecting our desires to Ireland, to the Middle and Far East; to Russia, South Africa and all oppressed peoples; to India and the third world where poverty and destitution bring men and women to the brink of despair; as well as to our own country where the corroding power of affluence and greed is a constant threat to that foundation on which all true religion rests, the sense of trust and hope in God.

There is nothing parochial in petitions such as these. They embody the aspirations of very many people at this time, including those who

1

are out of touch with any form of organised religion, that the love of God which is at the heart of the gospel committed to us shall find its due expression in political, social and economic justice. Only when these great issues have been commended to God are we allowed to look to our more immediate needs, 'give us this day our daily bread', still praying as members of a family—for 'us', and not for 'me'—and asking for all things temporal and spiritual to enable us to fulfil God's purpose. We pass on to ask for the forgiveness of our sins, a petition which concerns our relationship with God as well as with one another; and then to the last petition, in which we ask God not to allow us to be tried beyond our strength and to save us from evil in the testing fire of temptation. The Lord's Prayer is thus petitionary throughout. The apparent exception—the doxology—is of course not part of the original prayer, but an addition used by the early Church.

★ ★ ★ ★ ★ ★

If we pass on from the Lord's Prayer itself to our Lord's direct teaching on prayer we shall find that it is always the petitionary aspect of prayer which is expounded. In St Luke's gospel the Prayer is immediately followed by the parable of the householder who, on the untimely arrival of a guest, goes at midnight to a friend's house to beg for food, and refuses to allow any peace to the man or his family until this request is granted. The almost parallel story of the unjust judge also urges us to persist in prayer. This time we have a widow pestering a judge until he attends to her needs and grants her the justice she is seeking. In the further parable of the pharisee and the publican it is once again petitionary prayer that is commended, the publican's cry that God will be merciful to him as a sinner. So too, in our Lord's most commonly quoted teaching on prayer, 'Ask, and it shall be given you, seek, and you shall find, knock, and it shall be opened to you', petitionary prayer pure and simple is placed before us. After being reminded that God will give not less lavishly and lovingly than a human father, we are led to the climax that God will surely give the Holy Spirit to those who ask him.

When we turn from our Lord's teaching to consider his own prayers as they are recorded in the gospels, we find that these too are basically

2

petitionary. He prays for the soldiers, 'Father forgive them, for they do not know what they do', and for Peter, 'I have prayed for you that your faith may not fail'. He prays for the disciples, 'that they may be sanctified through the truth', and for the members of his Body, 'that they may all be one, even as, thou Father, art in me and I in thee, that they also may be one in us'. Finally we may recall the distress and anguish in Gethsemane, 'Father, if it be possible let this cup pass from me', leading on to petition at its most costly and sacrificial level, 'nevertheless, not my will but thine be done'.

What is true of the gospels is no less true of the epistles, where petition remains at the heart of prayer though, here too, purged of its selfish elements and ennobled by the fire of the Spirit. As an example of the grandeur and nobility to which such prayer may rise, let us take this passage from the Epistle to the Ephesians:

> I bow my knees before the Father from whom every family in heaven and earth is named, that according to the riches of his glory he may grant you to be strengthened with might through his Spirit in the inner man, and that Christ may dwell in your hearts through faith; that you, being rooted and grounded in love, may have power to comprehend with all the saints what is the breadth and length and height and depth, and to know the love of Christ which surpasses knowledge, that you may be filled with all the fullness of God.

It is the same with the Old Testament. The commentaries, of course, tell us that prayer in the Old Testament can be understood widely to include every form of address to God, whatever its character—and this is strictly true. Yet, with two exceptions only (the Prayer of Hannah and the reference at the end of Psalm 72 to 'the prayers of David the son of Jesse'), wherever the Old Testament uses the word prayer, it is the petitionary aspect that is referred to. It may be that, unthinkingly, we often limit petitionary prayer to such passages as the description of Solomon's prayer at the dedication of the temple, or Nehemiah's at its re-building after the exile. We overlook the petitionary nature of such well-known sentences as 'O Lord open thou our lips', or, 'O God make speed to save us'. It may surprise us to learn that in Psalm 119 alone there are no fewer than seventy petitions to God.

Is the point I am making, that prayer in the Bible is deeply rooted in petition, an academic one only? If I believed that I would not have laboured it. On the contrary, I believe it to be a point of immense practical importance, for it seems that here nothing less than personality in God is at stake. Once the concept of petition at the heart of prayer is surrendered, it will not be long before we relinquish the idea of God as personal—and that is a statement which could equally well be put the other way round. The conceptions of God as Father and of prayer as petitionary are no more separable than the two sides of a coin. In parenthesis let me add that I am conscious, even as I use the word, that to speak of God as 'personal' is deplorably inadequate. I should prefer to use some such word as 'supra-personal', but I can no more conceive what that means than I can conceive of a fourth dimension or a beginning and end of time. We call God 'He'—and 'She' would do just as well, because the pronoun is used to denote person and not gender—not in the sense in which we use 'he' of a friend, but because the limitations of language leave us with the personal pronoun as the only alternative to 'it'. If God were 'IT', with capital letters—the greatest, so to speak, of all possible 'its'—we should be his master and not he ours. 'He' can do no more than indicate that God has the power of initiative no less than we have, even though we may believe that he has vastly more. The doctrine of the Trinity, in itself a mystery, encourages us in the belief that a concept of the Godhead beyond the personal as we know it, is not without meaning.

But to return to our argument. Once we lose the concept of personality as applied to God it will not be long before we lose the concept of him as 'absolute demand' and so of ourselves as owing him 'total commitment'. That is probably the danger of what is generally called mystical religion when it is divorced from biblical theology. This can be seen in the East, where the biblical insights we have just been considering are largely foreign. It can be seen too in some of the esoteric cults springing up in the West today, orientated around some *guru*. The practice of religion becomes a matter of preference, like the choice of friends, and there is lacking the note of urgency, still more of obligation which is stamped on the prophetical and dominical approach. I do not of course mean to belittle mystical prayer—the faithful practice of silence, adoration, petition, may ultimately lead us into such prayer—but simply stressing the importance of basing our prayer on firm biblical foundations. Thomas Merton once wrote: 'The simplicity of the gospels, if kept in mind, makes false mysticism impossible. Christ has delivered us for ever from the esoteric and the strange. He has brought the light of God to our own level to transfigure our ordinary existence.'

CHAPTER II

A Difficulty Considered

READERS of this book will probably fall into two main groups. There will be those who conceive of God in terms which deny personality, regarding him (let the personal pronoun stand) as a sort of diffused, impersonal, spiritual energy pervading the universe. It would seem to follow that for such people prayer, as we have been regarding it, can have no place in their lives. They might perhaps hope to *use* God, that is to say, to harness this vast source of spiritual energy for the benefit of themselves and others; but to beseech him, to appeal to him, to invoke him—that would make no sense at all. You can harness the power of steam and use it for the propulsion of ships and trains, but you cannot address to steam the desires and aspirations of your heart.

The other group will include those of more or less orthodox Christian belief, people who affirm personality in the Godhead and who pray to God as Father. Yet amongst these it may be assumed there will be some who can find no place for petitionary prayer except, perhaps, as allowing a certain psychological benefit to those who know they are being prayed for. Having in mind the difficulties of this class, let us go on now to consider the objection they are likely to bring against petitionary prayer and, as we proceed, some of the values conserved in this realm of prayer may become clearer.

The objection would, I think, run on some such lines as these: 'I believe God to be perfect wisdom and perfect love. If he is all-wise he knows what is best. I should not like him to give what is second best, whether for myself or for anyone else, and if I prayed to him, I might be asking for just that. And anyway, if he is all-loving, surely he will give what is best without my asking him? Therefore I prefer to worship him, and to praise him, and to enter into silent communion with him, but not to ask him for anything, whether for myself or others. I leave it to him to give as he sees best.' This seems at first sight a not unreasonable argument, nor is it one presented exclusively by lukewarm or shallow people. It was, for example, one of the points held against Madame Guyon in her examination by the Roman Catholic Church, that her system of prayer allowed no place for petition or intercession.

The fallacy of the argument is that it considers only two possibilities: either God wills it, and therefore it will happen anyway; or else God doesn't will it, and therefore I must not pray for it—and presents them as a reason for not praying. But the argument has overlooked a third possibility, namely, that God may want this event to happen—this sick person, let us suppose, to recover—*in answer to our prayer*. Our line of reasoning has lost sight of the possibility that prayer may open a channel through which it becomes morally possible for God to work— as Father Raynes of the Community of the Resurrection used to say— not *changing* God's purpose, but *releasing* it.

The thought will be made clearer if we transfer our attention from the realm of prayer to that of action. Here then is a mother with her baby boy whose life depends on being fed at her breast. She reasons thus: 'God wants my child to live or he does not. If he wants him to live he will live anyhow, and I need not feed him. If he doesn't want him to live, it would be wrong of me to feed him. Either way I need do nothing,' The fallacy, painfully obvious in the realm of action, seems often to go undetected in the realm of prayer. God wants this child to live *through* the mother's co-operation, with all that this means to mother and child in establishing a relationship of dependence and love on which the healthy spiritual and psychological development of both depend. No basic change of principle is involved in God's dealing with men when we move from the sphere of action to that of prayer.

6

What has perhaps been unduly laboured here is summed up tersely by C. S. Lewis as follows:

'Praying for particular things,' said I, 'always seems like advising God how to run the world. Wouldn't it be wiser to assume that he knows best?' 'On the same principle', said he, 'I suppose you never ask the man next to you to pass the salt, because God knows best whether you ought to have salt or not. And I suppose you never take an umbrella because God knows best whether you ought to be wet or dry.' 'That's quite different', I protested. 'I don't see why', said he. 'The odd thing is that He should let us influence the course of events at all. But since He lets us do it in one way, I don't see why He shouldn't let us do it in another.'

Whether it be odd or not, it is certainly beyond dispute that God does allow us to direct to some extent the course of world history by our hands and feet and brains, these physical organs being but three among many which, as instruments of the human will, may influence the stream of events around us. When the atom bomb was dropped on Japan in 1945, bringing the war abruptly to an end, every country in the world felt in some measure the impact of that event. And God allowed this to come about through man—man's brain in designing 'that hideous strength', and man's body acting in co-ordination with his mind and will.

And yet, while it is true that God allows man an astonishing degree of freedom in shaping events for good or ill, that freedom is by no means absolute. Limitations are placed upon it—not necessarily for all time, for the domain under man's control progressively increases as nature yields up one secret after another. Where this will stop we have no means of knowing. Man can modify the weather by planting trees or cutting them down, or by firing chemicals into rain clouds, but he cannot control it to any extensive degree. Man can regulate the birth rate, but the sex of the unborn child is not—as yet—within his power to decide. Nor can he command the ebb and flow of the ocean tides. It is easy to see how human control over such things could lead to disaster, and we may be thankful that God in his wisdom has placed them, and much more besides, beyond our present powers. Yet these, and other examples we might take, serve to remind us of the astonishing range of freedom which he does allow.

If then, we may ask, God entrusts so much to us through the exercise of free will in the realm of action, would it not be strange if he should entrust nothing to us in the realm of prayer? We do not find any such division between action and speech—doing things and asking things— in ordinary family life. Each has its part to play in developing and deepening relationships in the home. The child will at one time express his heart's desire by action—playing cricket in the garden, romping with the dog, or making a model aeroplane—and at another time he will express it by speech, asking his father if they may go camping for the summer holidays this year. The father will not always agree to the boy's request, but it is through the expression of the will in action and speech that family relations are enabled to grow.

Our Lord encourages us to look to the family if we would discover the manner of God's dealing with us, and nowhere is this more true than in the realm of prayer. Surely it is just what we should expect— that the relationships proper to normal family life should have their counterparts among us who have received the spirit of adoption whereby we cry, 'Abba, Father'. It is the plain teaching of Jesus, that God our Father, in his love for us, wants us to look to him to supply our needs, whether temporal or spiritual, with the simplicity and faith of children, and to make known our requests boldly. It is true that he knows our needs before we ask him—we have our Lord's word for that— but prayer will prepare us to receive his gifts and use them in his service. Fellowship and communion will be taken to new depths and—a mark always of true discipleship—our lives will be irradiated by a spirit of thanksgiving.

To make a request to God in prayer does not mean that we are excused from working as far as we are able to bring about the end for which we have prayed. If we pray, 'Create in me a clean heart O God and renew a right spirit within me', we must order our lives as far as possible to that end. The way we live will be the test of the reality of the way we pray. The example chosen is a prayer for spiritual blessing, but prayer for material blessing is equally enjoined in the New Testament. Not only does our Lord teach us to pray for material blessings, but it is to such prayer that he responds in his healing miracles and he continues to confirm his teaching in the experience of men and women throughout the ages and not least in our own time.

★　　★　　★　　★　　★　　★

What then am I saying—that we may pray for whatever we want? We are certainly free to *take* all our desires to God in prayer. It may be that he will grant them, even when the things we seek are not what we might call his primary will for us, as a father might decide to allow a headstrong schoolboy son to be out at night even though he knew the boy's best interest (and thus his own primary will) lay in his remaining indoors and doing his homework. The Bible expresses that thought in Psalm 106, 'Lust came upon them in the wilderness and they tempted God in the desert. And he gave them their heart's desire and sent leanness withal into their soul.' Colin Morris has expressed it still more tersely in the words, 'Look out what you pray for—you may get it', adding that, to judge from the mess we are in, many people's *real* prayers—meaning by 'real prayer' the heart's desire and not necessarily the utterance of the lips—have indeeed been granted.

If, however, we are trying to be realistic and sincere in our Christian living, our basic desire will not be that God should bend his will to ours, but that through the discipline of prayer our wills may be brought into closer conformity with his—that he will cleanse the defective desires of our hearts by the inspiration of his Holy Spirit. This, for the committed Christian, is a continuing process, and he knows that, at each stage, what he looks to God to give him is likely to fall short of what God would have him receive, and so every prayer he makes is governed by the petition, 'thy will be done', whether explicitly expresssed or not. This means that we are prepared—or at least desire to be prepared—for anything, even if God's plans should drive a deep furrow across our own. The anonymous writer of the following words must have been well schooled in God's way of dealing with his people:

> So easily do we pray for the wrong things: for strength that we may achieve, and God gives us weakness that we may be humble; for health that we may do great things, and God gives us infirmity that

9

we may do better things; for riches that we may be happy, and God gives us poverty that we may be wise; for power that we may have the praise of men, and God gives us weakness that we may feel the need of him; for all things that we may enjoy life, and God gives us life that we may enjoy all things; and so, receiving nothing that we have asked for but all that we have genuinely hoped for, our prayer has been answered and we have been blessed.

Although often we shall not know how to pray as we ought, we shall naturally seek to avoid what may be called the forbidden areas of prayer. Prayers which often seem permissible when we view ourselves or others in isolation may become impossible when we reflect that we pray as members of a family in which the good of one may conflict with the interest of another. It is also important that our prayer shall specify 'open possibilities'. Here we are in some difficulty, but in practice all of us recognise that God has so ordered the world that some situations are open to prayer and others are closed. For example, most Christians would think it right to pray for a friend with a septic arm, presuming the situation to present an open possibility. If the arm had to be amputated, we should say God had declared himself (in respect, at least, of his permissive will) and our prayer would be directed to our friend's mental adjustment to his new state. But it isn't always easy to know what is open and what is closed. Sickness, for example, we should generally hold to be open; the weather some would probably regard as open and many as closed; the timing of the ebb and flow of the tides we should all regard as closed. But it is important to note that closed possibilities exist not because God's power is limited, but because, if the world were otherwise organised and disciplined, life as we know it would become impossible.

Considerations such as these show petitionary prayer to be a very different thing from what people out of touch with the Church sometimes *imagine* Christians believe it to be—a sort of Aladdin's lamp which we can so manipulate as to bring about our fondest wish. If that picture were to bear any resemblance to truth, the only condition under which chaos would not immediately ensue, would be if the lamp itself were in the hands of infinite wisdom and perfect love. and while it would be misleading to press the rather crude comparison any further—for God is a master lover, not a master magician—that is just where we would claim the lamp to be. At the same time, belief in God's sovereign control does not exclude the possibility of his allowing man a certain freedom in the realm of petitionary prayer—a freedom consistent with human love and wisdom indeed, but consistent also with God's power to say 'no' as well as 'yes'.

I find it much easier to understand the man who denies absolutely the existence of God than the man who, believing in the God and Father of our Lord Jesus Christ, makes him deny us any active co-operation with him in the realm of prayer. That prayer *does* effect new things—that certain events which would not otherwise have happened do happen as a result of prayer being offered—Christians must surely believe beyond all doubt. Yet, as we have seen, we need to balance this insight with another. We do not go to prayer that we may use God but that he may use us. We trust him to use our prayer as he wills in the extension of his blessing, and we trust him further to make us, through the discipline and training of prayer, more effective instruments of his will. One result of prayer will be to make us more fit to receive aright the good things, spiritual and material, which God wants to give. And prayer for one another will build us up into a fellowship of love, the deepest of all blessings, from which much else will flow.

CHAPTER III

Intercession and Miracle

INTERCESSORY prayers such as we are familiar with in church have both advantages and dangers. The advantages, as has well been said, are their theological depth and richness, their spiritual insight, their balance and beauty of language and their range, so far beyond what our own prayers are likely to compass. They give us a standard to which we may increasingly approximate, setting before us things of lasting value in place of the transient things on which we so easily set our hearts. But these are values into which we have to grow. 'When I use the Church's prayers', says Colin Morris, summing it all up in one colourful sentence, 'I feel like a small boy wearing his father's suit, hoping he will grow into it one day.'

But prayer is never just a matter of words. Its roots are in the desires of the heart. The act of speaking may often assist us in developing and expressing our inmost desires, but the words are a help to *us*, not to God. We should be warned also that words and phrases, however holy they may sound, cannot become prayer merely by being repeated. For prayer requires always an involvement of mind and heart and will, and wherever this is present in relationship with God, there will prayer be offered, whether words are said or not. Conversely, no verbal utterance without such involvement can be of the nature of prayer at all. When Christians pray as they are taught, 'Thy kingdom come', it may be that only for the saints of God are words and desires perfectly blended into one. For most of us, the words will express not so much our desire as it is as, rather, what we desire that it shall be. We desire indeed that God's kingdom shall come, but we do not desire it with the whole of ourselves. If when we pray we put the energies of our spirit, fervently yet unaffectedly into our words, then the words will help to kindle our hearts and bring utterance and desire into harmony. There is a danger, however, that words, instead of being an expression of the interior energies of the spirit may be used as a substitute for it. If so, they become a mockery—'vain repetition', as the Authorised Version has it in a pregnant phrase. People sometimes think that vain repetition means, simply, saying the same prayer over and over again. But this need not be so; the Jesus Prayer, for example, is a form of prayer which lends itself to continuous repetition, but it is far from being on that account vain. The reality of a prayer has nothing to do with the number of times it is repeated, but depends rather on the simplicity and truth in which it is made. A prayer repeated only once, if the heart is not engaged, is a vain repetition.

However helpful it may be to use words in intercessory prayer, we do well to remind ourselves they are not of its essence. We are familiar enough with this in everyday life. Collectors for charities do not usually speak to passers-by—holding out the box is itself a sufficient request. Suffragettes who chained themselves to railings knew that actions speak more eloquently than words. Equally, we may intercede by asking God to accept this or that activity as a prayer for the cause we have at heart. This is no soft option—it is, in fact, as costly as we choose to make it. Thus one person may get up early to make his Communion on behalf of a sick friend; another may do some piece of work; others again may deny themselves some pleasure or luxury, or make an offering of money to some representative cause—the possibilities are endless. There is no need to keep the friend or the cause in mind throughout such times, a simple act of intention is enough, together with an offering of heart and will to God of what we have chosen to do.

Commenting on Hebrews 7:25, 'He ever lives to make intercession for us', Bishop Michael Ramsey has said that the basic meaning of intercession is not pleading with God but standing in God's presence on behalf of another. And so, simply to hold another in the silence before God, may become for us the most important way of intercessory prayer. On such prayer John Austin Baker has an illuminating passage in his book *The Foolishness of God*:

When we pray for others we shall see that by far the most important requirement is inner calmness and tranquillity. We are not engaged in creating or producing anything, but in becoming aware of what is already the fact, namely that God is immediately and intimately present both to ourselves and to the one for whom we are praying. Our task is to hold the awareness of this in the still centre of our being, to unite our love for them with God's love, in the quiet but total confidence that he will use our love to help bring about the good in them which we both desire. In technical terms, therefore, intercession is a form of that kind of prayer known as 'contemplation', with the special feature that here we contemplate not God in himself but God in his relationship of love to those whom we also love; and on the basis of our partnership with him we entrust our love into his hands to be used in harness with his own for their benefit.

★　★　★　★　★　★

It has been said earlier that many people would be prepared to defend prayer only at what might be called the psychological level. They would say, for example, that John's knowledge that Paul is praying for him in his sickness will be a comfort and strength, and an assurance that he is loved and cared for. Probably they would add that this knowledge might help John towards a new hope and courage, which in turn would be likely to react upon his bodily condition, so that the prayer offered would indeed assist his return to health. Certainly no Christian would be concerned to deny that this is one of the ways in which petitionary prayer acts. Nor, if he is wise, will he belittle its importance. But he will be bound to admit that to restrict the operation of prayer to some such mode as this fails completely to do justice to the teaching of Our Lord and of the New Testament as a whole, to the witness of the early church and indeed to the Church's experience in every age, including the present. When Our Lord said to blind Bartimaeus, 'Receive your sight', or when St Peter said to the cripple at the gate of the temple, 'In the name of Jesus Christ of Nazareth stand up and walk', we are in the presence of a new creation—what takes place can in no sense be explained subjectively within the terms of raising a man's morale. We are in the presence of a miracle.

I think it ought to be said that belief in miracle does not mean we believe that God, in answer to prayer, will suspend or change natural laws on which the orderly ruling of the universe depends. If a child were to fall over a precipice the natural result would be for gravity to pull him to the ground. But if his father by an act of will stretches out his hand, grabs his son and pulls him back to safety, no one imagines the law of gravity to have been susupended—we simply recognise that a new force, projected into the situation, has had its way. So too, when our Lord walked on the water there was no suspension of the law of gravity, but a new power was interposed by the divine will. The point is expressed as follows by Bishop Reichel (quoted in A. L. Worlledge's book, *Prayer*):

> The intervention of the divine will in answer to prayer, by simply directing the energies and powers of nature to a result which, if left undirected, they would not have arrived at, seems to me, on the most careful reflection, just as possible as that of which we see the results in every part of the globe at every moment—I mean the intervention of the human will, not in the way of 'suspending' or 'superseding', but in the way of using the laws of nature by directing natural forces into certain channels.

We note that the quotation begins with the words 'the intervention of the divine will', and it is that which is always the essential element of miracle. In his booklet, *Our Understanding of Prayer*, the late Bishop Ian Ramsey of Durham makes the same point, though rather more cautiously, in these words:

> Prayer undoubtedly supposes that it makes sense to speak of God's activity as directed to a particular point and as effecting something new in the universe. Does it? We all know how human effort can change the world and how by thought and skill we can create novelty in town and country. It is true that in our case this needs the intervention of our bodily organism. But if God is related to the whole universe in the way described earlier—on the analogy of ourselves to our bodies—this may still be a profitable reflection. In general terms we are only required to believe in principle that God can act within the texture of the universe, and certainly the Christian can have no fundamental difficulty with this concept. The Christian certainly

cannot in principle exclude God's special activity in Christ from being effective in nature and human nature.

In his book *The World and God* another writer, Dr H. H. Farmer, lists three elements which he holds to be indispensable to miracle:

> First, there is an awareness of serious crisis, or need, or threat of disaster in the personal life, and of helplessness to deal with it adequately and victoriously through the exercise of ordinary, unaided powers. Second, there is a more or less conscious and explicit turning to God for assistance. Third, there is an awareness of an *ad hoc* response to God, to the situation and to man's petitionary inadequacy in it, so that the crisis is met, the need satisfied, the danger averted in an event, or combination of events, which would not have taken place had not man so petitioned and God so acted.

Miracle then involves a special breaking in of God to the world, and in the sense in which Dr Farmer uses the term, this comes about in answer to man's prayer. We have ordinarily no means of knowing how often this may happen, or indeed, when it does happen that it has done so in answer to some specific prayer—God, after all, does know our needs before we ask him. But for my own part I do not require proof in order to believe that we are covered with divine or angelic protection much more frequently than we are likely to be aware.

I do not know how well-known is the following story about the beloved Bishop of Lincoln, Edward King, but I tell it as I remember hearing it from a younger member of the family. The Bishop was walking alone one night along one of the lonely fen roads outside Lincoln to visit a sick person to whom he had been called. When he arrived at the cottage he found no one ill, nor could anyone explain the message. The matter might have ended there but, some years later, a condemned murderer whom the Bishop had prepared for confirmation told him that it was he who had sent the message, that he had been lying in wait in the ditch to assault and rob him, when he had seen to his surprise that the bishop was not alone but was flanked by a man on either side.

Even a Christian so much aware of spiritual realities as Bishop King would have remained unconscious of divine protection but for this

16

unexpected sequel; and there may still be left in the story an element unrevealed—a prayer offered specially for the Bishop's safety. If we go strictly by Dr Farmer's definition some such such petition would seem necessary if we are to call the episode a miracle. But in my view it is miraculous as it stands. We do not know just how God may have protected us, not only—or even chiefly—from bodily harm, but from spiritual dangers which might have quite overwhelmed us, nor to what extent other people's prayer may have been instrumental in this. No doubt the visible evidence of angelic protection such as this story illustrates is of rare occurrence, but it is legitimate to wonder how much of what we generally call coincidence, or chance, or luck, may not be due to a special providence of God.

★　　★　　★　　★　　★　　★

The question naturally arises that if God can, and often does, intervene, why does he not do so more often? What are we to make of the car accidents, the plane crashes, the tragic shootings and the whole field of disaster with which our papers are so largely filled, as well as the daily onset of fatal illness and sudden death? No definite answer can ever be given to such questions, but there are certain reflections that have to be made.

The first of these is that God did not intervene to save his own Son from suffering and death on the cross, though he might have done so. Even after the decisive victory of Gethsemane, Jesus is fully aware that the way of deliverance is still open. 'Do you think', he asks the soldiers who arrest him, 'that I cannot appeal to my Father and he will at once send me more than twelve legions of angels?' But that appeal was never made. The really breathtaking aspect of God's love in the Incarnation is the self-emptying and humiliation, leading to the anguish of Gethsemane and Calvary where our Lord took on himself all the suffering man can experience, and more. The theoretical problem of suffering may remain, but in the power of the Spirit it is seen to be transcended and taken into the redemptive purpose of God. A Christian sees God working from within every tragedy and occasion of suffering which, in union with Christ, become experiences that are redemptive for the world itself.

Brother Edward, pioneer of the Village Evangelists, expresses this in one of his letters:

> I do seriously believe that all suffering patiently endured is linked with the one suffering of Christ in redeeming the world. I believe that if I can suffer bravely and put faith and courage and love into it, that suffering of mine will count towards the world's salvation. I believe that actually those who suffer in the Spirit are, under Christ, our greatest and most generous benefactors. They do more for us than the busiest who bustle about in service.

A further reflection is that there must be, in regard to God's special intervention, a great economy of action. If God were to interfere in every situation where we got ourselves into difficulties, all controlled, disciplined and planned life would be at an end. If no fire broke out when the children upset the oil stove, if the aircraft didn't fall when the mechanic had failed to tighten a vital nut, and if the same absence of risk were to be found in every department of life, there could be no incentive to carefulness, responsibility, order, discipline. Moreover, every future event would be unpredictable, and planning, in any free human sense, impossible. It is because we are set in a framework of natural law which normally goes unhampered on its own majestic course, that life as a school and training ground for character can exist at all. If life were studded with miracles comparable to the stilling of the storm and the feeding of the five thousand, man, at his present stage of moral development, would be lost. When these things happen once or twice in a lifetime, they serve to reveal the autonomy of God's creative power and to awaken adoration and trust. When the Queen visits a school a week's holiday is given. The school can absorb that because there is only one queen and she is not likely to return in the next hundred years—no school could survive a monthly royal visit and no economic system could survive a frequent multiplication of loaves.

Yet as a final consideration, can we be sure that we ought to wish for miracles even if we saw them as possibilities? Many people think of miracle as a reward of man's faith. We forget it may equally be a concession to his weakness. The stilling of the storm is just such a case. Our Lord's primary will for the disciples was not that they should be spared the ordeal of the storm, but that they should meet it with untroubled hearts, in serenity and trust. Hence he rebuked not merely the winds and the waves, but the panic-stricken men whose faith had failed. Those who have grasped the values and priorities of the kingdom will know that its deepest rewards are found where troubles, distresses, calamities, disappointments—whatever form the storm may take—have been accepted and passed through lovingly and trustfully in God's saving grace. This does not mean that God's succour, in whatever way it is present, is not to be accepted. It would be presumption on our part to think we know best how our deliverance should be brought about, but the whole tenor of the New Testament is that we should normally expect deliverance *through*—and not *from*—trial and affliction. The reward for the man who has built his house upon the rock of the gospel is not that it shall be protected from the batterings of nature but, that after the rains have fallen and the floods have risen and the winds have blown, it shall remain firm. In the words of Mother Julian, 'He said not *thou shalt not be tempested* but *thou shalt not be overcome*'.

CHAPTER IV

Four Preliminaries to Contemplation

THE FIRST POINT, which governs all that I shall have to say, is that life must be taken and accepted as a whole, and prayer can never be separated from life, except for the purpose of analysis. Of course, a good deal depends on how we define prayer. Some people speak of prayer as if to equate it with Christian living. Their way of praying, they would say, is caring for old people or visiting the sick in hospital. If we choose to enlarge our definition of prayer in this way we must allow it also to include washing-up and gardening, earning a living and travelling to work, doing the crossword, eating, drinking and sleeping. The whole range of life will be included. And we should indeed be on shaky ground if we were to claim greater value in the sight of God for any one of these activities rather than another; for the value of any work resides not in the nature of the work itself, but in the love which inspires us to respond to God in whatever he calls us to do. In *The Practice of the Presence of God*—a little book but a great spiritual classic—Brother Lawrence saw, with true insight, how all perfection could be contained in such a simple act as picking up a straw off the ground, if only it were done solely for the love of God. Such an action would be a purer form of prayer than the performance of some work beneficial to society but lacking the motivation of love. *Though I give all my goods to feed the poor, and though I give my body to be burned and have not love . . .*

Now whilst I am fully prepared to go along with this view which sees prayer as co-extensive with Christian living, and to agree further that in holding it one holds also to some important principles—it does away, for example, with a false antithesis between secular and religious— yet clearly it is not a view of prayer which will serve my purpose in writing this book. For by adopting it I should commit myself to writing on the whole range of Christian life rather than on one specific activity within it. In the following pages we shall be regarding prayer as the activity in which we are engaged when, alone or in company with others, our hearts and minds and wills are occupied with God and with him alone; and we shall regard all other activity, whether 'religious' or 'secular' as the overspill of that prayer into the daily life of the Christian. God is to be glorified in the whole of our life, but this is only likely to happen if we ensure that there are regular times in which we seek him and only him, times in which every motive other than the glory of God is, as far as may be, excluded. God does not value our prayer time because it is in itself more valuable than other times, but because the other times should be charged with the significance of this particular time. The point has been well summarised by John Dalrymple in his book *The Christian Affirmation*—'You are never likely to be able to pray everywhere all the time', he says, unless you first learn to pray somewhere some of the time.'

But in so limiting the activity of prayer we must remember that it is never to be disengaged from the total offering of life. It is the risk that this may happen—and in fact sometimes does—that has so often brought the subject of prayer into disrepute. And so we must stress like a thread that runs through all our thinking, the principle that prayer can never be sealed off in a compartment on its own. Prayer and life will be continually acting and reacting on one another. Insofar as our daily work is not open to the impulse and direction of the Holy Spirit, to that extent will our prayer life be weakened; and conversely, insofar as there is a holding back or want of openness in our prayer life, to that extent will the work we offer to God be enfeebled. Dedication in our prayer life without a corresponding dedication in our work can be no more than an appearance—it is our work that tests the reality of our prayer. Naturally it will take time for prayer to permeate the whole but ultimately, all aspects of life will move towards a deeper consecration, each supporting and encouraging the other.

★　　★　　★　　★　　★　　★

The second point which underlies all that we shall be saying is that only the Holy Spirit can teach us how to pray. That is so obvious as to be almost trite—we hear it again and again, we meet it in all the books and, perhaps for just that reason, we pay it less attention than we should. We can of course find help and direction from books and from people, but in the end, prayer is the work of the Holy Spirit within us and he alone is our teacher. The Spirit, says St Paul, comes to the aid of our weakness. We do not even know how we ought to pray, but 'the Spirit himself makes intercession for us with groanings that cannot be uttered'. Here perhaps we are coming close to a definition of contemplative prayer—'Groanings which cannot be uttered', 'sighs too deep for words' (in the RSV) or, in the paraphrase supplied by one of the commentaries, 'inexpressible longings which God alone understands'. Contemplation is indeed a gift, the gift of the Spirit which only he can impart and only he can develop within us. It should be sought by waiting rather than by effort, gently, and with a patience that abides God's time rather than urging our own desires. The Spirit moves where he wills, and whether he moves us to pray vocally, to 'speak with tongues' or to be silent in contemplation, he alone is our teacher and guide.

Many years ago when I was about twenty-four, I remember going for a walk with Father Wigram, the Superior at that time of the Cowley Fathers at St Edward's House in Westminster and a man of considerable spiritual stature. Bede Frost's book, *The Art of Mental Prayer*, had recently been published and was enjoying a good deal of popularity. At the heart of the book there are descriptions of the various methods of meditation—the Oratorian, Carmelite, Ignatian, Franciscan and others. I should be unable to say much about them now, but I had read the book at the time and no doubt said a good deal. We were nearing the end of our walk when I turned to my companion and said, 'And Father, how do you pray?' A few moments' silence and then he said, 'Well, I usually kneel down and hope for the best'. It was a rebuke I well deserved, though not perhaps intended as such—the saints have a way of making devastating remarks with artless simplicity. To kneel down and hope for the best is good advice if we see hope as a theological virtue, along with faith and charity, the confident expectation that God the Holy Spirit will complete within us the good work he has begun. And with every period of prayer this process is carried forward. It has taken me many years to learn to kneel down and hope for the best. Let us not forget the place of freedom and simplicity in prayer.

★　　★　　★　　★　　★　　★

But to say that is not to imply that prayer, like every other activity, does not have its own technique. And here is the third point I wish to make. The word 'technique' may seem an inappropriate one to apply to prayer, but the fact that it can be misused should not deter us from securing its proper use. People sometimes say, and especially nowadays when *gurus* are being increasingly sought out in the western world, that prayer is some form of technique. That is an error as far, at least, as Christian prayer is concerned, and needs to be refuted. But the place of technique within the life of prayer is quite another matter and one we should be foolish to neglect. The end of prayer is encounter with the living God—communion, or fellowship, as we may equally call it—and technique must always be subordinate to encounter. As I write these words I am hoping for encounter—I hope that my spirit may commune with my readers' spirits and to that end I must use a technique, in this case, that of writing words in the English language.

A few years ago I was asked to give a talk to some Sisters in a convent in France. They knew little English and I knew less French and so, as the technique was poor, the encounter was spoilt. Of course there is a difference when it is God we are speaking to, for God looks not at the outward forms but at the heart and thus the outward forms, of which language is one and posture another, become matters of indifference. So I think we must say that technique is important from *our* point of view, but not from God's. Have you ever watched yourself or a friend speaking on the telephone? We nod our head up and down, shake it from side to side, we may clinch a point by making a gesture with our free arm—all of which may look a bit foolish since we are speaking to someone who cannot see us, but is both reasonable and sensible if it enables us to communicate better. So too, if technique helps us to pray better, there is no reason to despise it.

Later we shall enquire how technique relates to posture, and the correlation between tension and relaxation in different parts of the body. More attention has been paid to this in the non-Christian East than in the West. The truth is that you can approach a matter of this sort in two ways. Take, for example, the relationship of sleep to posture. Suppose you are out for a picnic and you fall asleep, your body will at once take up a posture suited to sleep— horizontal on the ground. But you could also start from the other end and say to yourself, 'Now that I want to go to sleep, I shall first lie down on the ground and then, given the desire for sleep, it will soon overtake me'. You have the same choice in prayer—in contemplative prayer the body will tend to assume the posture best suited to that state, but equally, if we consciously take up the position most conducive to prayer then, as prayer is what we intend and want, prayer will come. To many people that may sound artificial and mechanical applied to prayer. Yet every night, in regard to sleep, we first take the correct posture and then let sleep overtake us— and there is no difference in principle between the two. Of course the Holy Spirit alone can enable us to pray, but that need not prevent our taking a posture which will assist his action in us. There is still, it is true, the danger of mistaking the outer form for the inner reality but this can be overcome if we are alert and ready for it.

★   ★   ★   ★   ★   ★

As my fourth and final point in this chapter, I want to stress the importance of regarding prayer as an offering. This is especially true of the prayer of praise and thanksgiving, and of waiting upon God in silence. The psalmist says, 'I will offer unto God the sacrifice of thanksgiving and will call upon the name of the Lord.' The same thought is given a Christian content by the author of the Letter to the Hebrews who writes, 'Through Jesus let us continually offer up to God the sacrifice of praise, that is, the tribute of lips which acknowledge his name.' Our offering in prayer is to be linked with the offering of Jesus, in virtue of which we are reconciled to God, and so may offer ourselves as sons to their Father. We are enabled to make this offering not of ourselves but through the prevenient action of the Holy Spirit. Yet the offering *is* ours, for God does not override our freedom—it is ours as a response to grace, gladly and freely given. And since it is made through Jesus, we shall find encouragement in remembering that it cannot be made on its own, but is a part of the total offering of his mystical body the Church.

If we are able to see prayer quite simply in this way, as an offering, one important consequence will follow. We shall be relieved of all anxiety to make a 'success' of prayer, whatever that may mean. This in turn will save us from the discouragement which is perhaps the commonest reason why people do not persevere in their life of prayer. What we are doing in silent prayer often appears at the time to be futile and, since this *is* only an appearance, one of the soundest pieces of advice for anyone who is finding prayer difficult is, never to judge by how it seems to be at the time but only—if at all—by its later fruits. If our whole concern is to offer our prayer to God, we need not bother with the questions that arise in our minds—'Is this prayer helping me or anyone else? Is it strengthening? Is it helping my troubled mind and emotions?' Ignore such thoughts. Offerings were never meant to help or strengthen or do anything except be offered. We leave our offerings confidently and lovingly in God's hands; we do not demand that this or that should come of them. If we can offer our prayer with this kind of simplicity we shall be delivered from the one great enemy of prayer, subjectivity—those sideways glances at ourselves to see how we are getting along—and our lives will come to be more and more deeply rooted and grounded in God. We have already seen how praying and doing react upon one another and so, of course, what has been said about offering applies also to our daily work. The important thing about work is not that it should be a 'success' but that it should be whole-heartedly offered, and it will be helpful to recall that thought from time to time. But I believe we are likely to see this dimension of our work only if we are learning to see it in our prayers.

Offerings can, of course, go wrong. Some time ago a family in India sent me a gift of sweets. It came out of a background of poverty we in the western world would find hard to imagine, and when the parcel reached me the contents were spoilt and had to be thrown away. But the value of the offering, lying not in the substance of the gift but in the love which prompted it, remains unchanged. So with our prayers— of little worth in themselves, they are yet accepted for love's sake. These are very simple thoughts, but we cannot be too simple before God, and if we keep them in mind we will be helped by them.

Some people, however, are worried by this idea of prayer as offering—it suggests to them the picture of an eastern potentate delighting in the homage of his subjects. But that is a false picture and a quite arbitrary one, for God is not to be compared with an oriental monarch but with a father. A father takes delight in his child's offering not because it inflates his ego but because, through the total action, the relationship of father and son is enlarged and enhanced and it is in this progress of love that the father rightly delights. Father Benson of Cowley once wrote,

God appointed prayer . . . not because he had any delight in our formal homage but because he desired, by forming in us the habit of prayer, to draw us to look to himself, the fountain of all good.

As John Macquarrie has said in his book *Paths in Spirituality*, 'The glorification of God and the sanctification of man are not competing motives in worship.' And he quotes St Irenaeus as presenting in a few words the paradox which is always present in the situation of worship: 'The glory of God is a living man; and the life of man consists in beholding God.'

CHAPTER V

The Divine Office and the Jesus Prayer

WE ARE perhaps accustomed to think of contemplative prayer as belonging to those times when we kneel or sit or stand in silence in the presence of God. Certainly the heart's silence is of the essence of such prayer, but this does not necessarily mean the absence of words, and there will be many times when the recitation of the divine office or some other form of vocal prayer, such as the rosary, will reveal themselves as contemplative in nature. Often, for example, in saying the psalms of the office we may be drawn beyond the words to the very heart of prayer, our attention no longer on the words but on God himself. Father Augustine Baker, the seventeenth-century author of *Holy Wisdom*, a classic of spiritual direction, says that vocal prayer was 'ordained to this end, to supply and furnish the soul that needs with good matter . . . by which it may be united to God'.

The words of the office thus become the framework of our prayer and are there to support us when we need them. Here is a simple illustration. As I look out of my window, I see a large and rather old pheasant on the lawn. It runs gaily along the ground, takes a short flight and then, being tired, returns to the earth; then a little more running, another flight, and so on. It occurs to me that the recitation of the office can be rather like that. We move steadily along from verse to verse of the psalms, and then there may be a short period, as it were on the wing, when the words, though still recited, recede into the background and we are somehow taken beyond them and held for a few moments in that stillness which is God. And then—and this too is the point—just as our pheasant had the good solid earth to return to and support him as he moved forward again, so we have the words of the office to return to and be our support. The bird could not just fall into a void, and in the same way the words of the office prevent us falling back into the distracting and discordant imagery which often holds our minds.

We might well have approached the office from another angle. Indeed, it would have been more natural to do so. I have not because I wished to show how the office might be a way in to contemplative prayer—little bursts of it like the bird's little bursts of flight. But before the office does this for us, the repetition of its words, with due attention paid to them as the Spirit empowers us, can be a tremendous help in enabling us to collect our minds, and to leave behind the distractions and concerns and perplexities of life which so often scatter our mental and spiritual energy. That is primary for all of us, and if I did not mention it first it is because I assume we can understand it for the purposes of our present discussion.

It will help to make what I am saying more clear if you will picture to yourself three parallel horizontal lines. The middle line stands for the words of the office. The line below stands for the distracting occupations of daily living from which the words of the office, acting as the agent of the Spirit, continually draw our minds upwards; while the top line stands for contemplative prayer where the Spirit will at times take us beyond the words into the stillness which is God. Note that we are taken; we do not make the leap ourselves. It just happens as we go on our way, while the words remain to support us as we may need them.

Yet we have to be realistic and say that for one reason and another the daily office has largely dropped out of the worshipping life of the Church and that the opportunities which were open to people of an older generation are less often available today. There are encouraging signs of a renewed desire for this aspect of the Church's worship and perhaps the situation will change again. Meanwhile what I have said is not wasted because the underlying principles apply to another form of vocal prayer to which it seems many are called today, and which can also be a way in to contemplative silence.

Many Christian people, though they probably will not speak of it unless it be to one or two like-minded friends, use some sort of vocal prayer frequently repeated such as the Jesus Prayer, which was made known to the Western world largely through *The Way of a Pilgrim*, first published in English about fifty years ago. Perhaps this book is the best introduction to the prayer, for we there meet it kindled in a human heart.* Its full form is, 'Lord Jesus Christ, Son of the Living God, have mercy on me a sinner.' But it has various shorter forms and can be reduced to the oft-repeated single word, 'Jesus'. It is not of course just an exercise of the lips. Far from it! The heart and mind will be, in a very simple and unstrained way, enfolded in what is being said.

I should only want to commend this prayer to those who have a special drawing to it. But I think some form of repetitive vocal prayer (with cautions against indiscriminate use which we shall come to later), is likely to be a help to many who have not yet found the Jesus Prayer. The psalms, of course, supply an inexhaustible treasury: 'Praise the Lord O my soul, and all that is within me praise his holy name'; 'Make me a clean heart O God, and renew a right spirit within me'; 'Be still and know that I am God.' Equally, we could take something much longer, such as a psalm known by heart, or a collect, or verses of a hymn. Whatever it is thus becomes to us *our* office, and like the offices of the Church not only does it preserve us from a dissipation of our energies (recall those three parallel lines), but it is a launching pad for the silent prayer of the heart. It has to be used with discretion and there can be a danger of a zeal which outruns wisdom. It is always good if we can turn to some experienced person with whom we can discuss these things. In using such prayers what is important is to mean 'God', and to go on meaning God—whether the actual words at any particular moment seem to have meaning for us or not. When the words fade away into the background, we can still mean God beyond the words.

Here we return to the question of vain repetition. Let me put it

*For another excellent description of this way see the chapter, 'The Prayer of the Name' in *Prayer* by Abhishiktananda (SPCK), a French Benedictine monk who made his home in India. See also *The Power of the Name* by Kallistos Ware (SLG Press) which is probably the finest short exposition of this prayer written in the last few years (1974, revised edition 1977).

another way. Hammering can be vain repetition if the nail moves not a fraction of an inch, but if each blow takes it, even minutely, nearer its destination, the hammering is no longer vain. So too, if every repetition of prayer helps to unite us, however little, more closely with God who is the end of all prayer, the repetition is not vain but profitable. It is right to go gently with this form of prayer, keeping it within our means and using it for perhaps not more than ten minutes at a time at first; we can then see how we are taken on from there.

The Jesus Prayer is particularly associated with the Eastern Orthodox tradition, and it is therefore in the classical collection of spiritual writings known as the *Philokalia* that we should look for advice concerning its use. And here we find stress laid, not once but a number of times, on what is called 'bringing the mind into the heart'—a phrase that applies equally well to the Jesus Prayer and to various other forms of words. We are helped to learn this by looking mentally towards the heart and, as we do so, we find after a time that for short periods the prayer becomes, as it were, lodged in the heart and will go on for a while of its own accord. In a beautiful little book on *The Invocation of the Name of Jesus* (published by the Fellowship of St Alban and St Sergius) a lovely likeness is drawn between this form of prayer and the flight of a bird, it may be that of an eagle. Through the measured beating of her wings the great bird ascends steadily higher and higher into the upper reaches of the air. Then for a time the wings are spread and still as she glides in graceful flight. Presently, when height has been lost, the motion of the wings begins again. So with our prayer, whatever form it takes, the actual repetition of the words will ebb and flow and yet, for those practised in it, the prayer itself will be ever carried in the heart. What matters in life beyond all else is that the mind and heart of man be stayed on God—whether we call this habitual recollection, prayer without ceasing, or something else—and only insofar as it serves that end is repetitive prayer to be cherished and practised.

A note of warning is needed here, however, because this form of prayer, used indiscriminately, can stir the unconscious levels of the mind beyond our immediate capacity to deal with them. It has been powerfully and cogently said that 'the pain of deepening self-knowledge is to be kept not at a bearable minimum, nor at an intolerable maximum,

C

but at a creative optimum'. Interpret that packed sentence in relation to food and then transfer it to the realm of prayer. In eating, there is a creative optimum, the amount which best suits us for our daily work. Below that there is a bearable minimum, but this leaves us too weak adequately to meet life's demands. And above it is an intolerable maximum which over-taxes the digestion and provides the body with more than it can assimilate. So too, at every stage, there is a right proportion in prayer. However, with that caution, let it be said that the need is more generally to stimulate and encourage the timid than to restrain the over-confident. Some of my readers will have known this way of prayer for a long while; to others it may be new. I would suggest to these latter: if your heart warms to this way of prayer and you feel a desire to embark on it, then in all probability the Holy Spirit is leading you to test it for a while. But if what has been said makes no appeal, then equally you may be fairly sure that this is not your way, at least for the present—and, indeed, many people are taken on into silent contemplation without experiencing this type of vocal prayer as a stage in their spiritual life.

Yet we are still only on the threshold of our subject. What I have been describing is perhaps best seen as a 'way in' to contemplative prayer. Often it forms a sort of passage from one type of prayer of which we do not hear very much today though it was widely practised in the past—the prayer of meditation. We shall not spend long on this but it is worth saying a few words. As Christians use the word (Eastern religions use it in a different sense), meditation means, basically, taking some passage, usually from the Bible, reading it, pondering over it, considering what bearing it has upon one's own life and one's relationships with others, and forming some resolution pertaining to the theme; at the end there will be free prayer of some kind. The Bible Reading Fellowship offers one of the many schemes available to those whose prayer is along these lines. It is thus that many of us have been launched on our prayer life and if we find such a pattern fruitful we should continue to follow it. Let me add that the way of contemplation does not mean there is no longer a place for the meditative hearing and reading of scripture and other books relating to the faith. What it does mean is that we shall find these occupations now do no more than touch the fringe of what we might call our real prayer.

For there comes a time in the lives of many people when this way of meditation is no longer satisfying. Even more, it becomes very difficult, indeed practically impossible, for them to follow it in their times of prayer. If this development is accompanied by a deep longing for God, if we find ourselves just wanting him and him alone, then we may take this as an indication that the Holy Spirit is leading us on into contemplative prayer, and we must be content to leave discursive meditation behind and yield to the prompting of the Spirit. 'Like as the hart desireth the water brooks, so longeth my soul after thee, O God.' 'When I awake after thy likeness I shall be satisfied.' Aspirations such as these, whether constant or recurring, may be taken as sure signs of the call to contemplation. At the same time, everyday things will very probably become less satisfying than before and there may be some withdrawal on our part, but in the end we are likely to come back to all the good things of God's creation, though now in a different way—now they will be caught up in the love of God and in the overflow of our prayer into the whole of daily life.

★   ★   ★   ★   ★   ★

What I am describing is, of course, a well-trodden path on the pilgrimage of the spirit. St John of the Cross is a reliable authority here and three times in his writings he points to the signs of this development. Many readers will recognise it as a stage in their own life, perhaps experienced many years ago. But, just as when you are motoring without a map and find yourself in unfamiliar country, you think anxiously that you may have lost the way, so some people for whom their former ways of prayer are no longer possible, become worried and discouraged, and because the silent ways in which they are now being led involve so much simplification of memory and mind and will, they may begin to ask whether they are praying at all. Very possibly they now try to turn back to the old way and, finding it fruitless, are tempted to give up altogether. This is where knowledge of the well-tried paths of the spirit can reinforce our faith and enable us to persevere. What is happening has been neatly summarised by Father Stanton in a short definition by which he distinguishes meditation from contemplation: 'Meditation is a detachment from the things of the world in order to attend to the things of God. Contemplation is a detachment from the things of God in order to attend to God himself.'

Before we go further we ought to make it clear that this silence of which we are speaking is not the silence of blankness or idleness, which has nothing to do with the drawing of the Holy Spirit. There are two images we might use to describe it. Think of a sentry on duty, an image of silence as alertness or awareness; or think of two people who love one another deeply, an image of silence as understanding and perception and harmony. We all know how different silences can be. There can be an idle silence or an embarrassed silence—better than either of these is conversation, in which we try to develop an awareness of one another's needs and interests. But that is only a stage (just as discursive meditation is only a stage), and sooner or later there will be a break-through and long periods can then pass, perhaps before the fire of a winter's evening, when each is supported by the silent presence of the other and conversation is superfluous or, rather, both are free to let it come or go at will. That is the picture of contemplative silence.

In approaching contemplative prayer in this way, I do not want to imply that people nowadays are generally drawn to contemplation through the earlier discipline of meditation. Historically speaking this is no doubt true, but formal meditation is much less taught and practised today and the contemplative call is likely to be a direct one. Anyone who finds within his heart an answering cry to St Augustine's great words, 'Thou hast made us for thyself and the heart of man is restless till it finds rest in thee', and who is ready in the grace of God to face the testing experiences of that quest should go forward, nothing doubting, on the path to which the Spirit is now calling him.

CHAPTER VI

Contemplation and the Cloud of Unknowing

IN PURSUIT of our study of contemplation we will now turn to a book which has very much come into its own in our day, the fourteenth-century *Cloud of Unknowing*. It is available in various editions both medieval and modern, but for practical purposes I would recommend the Penguin version in present-day English. In a valuable introduction the translator, Clifton Wolters, describes the anonymous author as a man of 'well-stored and scholarly mind, with a flair for expressing complexities simply,' and he goes on to say:'There was more than a streak of the poet in him, and at the same time a saving sense of humour and proportion. Probably most people will feel that they would like to know him, and some at least might wish they could have his guidance today.' This is what I propose we now seek.

The Cloud was written to a young disciple who had, it seems, appealed to the author for training in prayer. Through him it is addressed to a larger public, and yet by no means to everybody nor even to every devout Christian, but only to those who, by the inner working of the Spirit, God has disposed towards contemplation. We have already considered what constitutes that disposition.

Chapter Three begins, 'Lift up your heart to God with humble love and mean God and not what you get out of him.' Here at the very start we are reminded of a suggestion I made earlier that we should try to see prayer as an offering. Now part of that offering must be the offering of time, and about this we must be clear from the outset. It is almost too obvious to need saying that if there is to be prayer there must be time set apart for prayer. I am not suggesting that this is easy in an ordinary household, but I believe it would have to be an extraordinary household for it to be impossible. But once the time is set aside and adhered to, the battle is more than half won. The fact is that prayer is so much like hard work that most of us find that very ordinary things like writing a letter or making a telephone call take on an exaggerated importance when the time for prayer comes round. But to continue: 'Hate to think of anything but God himself, so that nothing occupies your mind or will but only God. Try to forget all created things . . . let them go, pay no attention to them . . . Do not give up but work away . . . When you first begin you find only darkness and a cloud of unknowing . . . Reconcile yourself to wait in this darkness as long as necessary, but go on longing after him you love . . . '; and again, 'strike that thick cloud of unknowing with the sharp dart of longing love and on no account think of giving up.'

Let us make a brief pause here. We have taken up our position for prayer, we have called upon the Holy Spirit, vocally or in the silent language of the heart, and we are now to let everything go, our thoughts, our imaginations, our memories, everything except this one thing that remains—and here is a phrase which keeps recurring in *The Cloud*—'a naked intention towards God and him alone'. The one thing necessary, we are told, is to 'mean God who created you and bought you and graciously called you to this state of life.

But how can we retain this intention in practice? We shall almost certainly need some simple thought as a focal point for the mind, and so the author allows us a word such as 'God', or 'love', or some other word given to us. This word he says is to be 'fixed fast to the heart' (and here we are reminded of the teaching in the *Philokalia* about 'bringing the mind into the heart') so that, our author continues, 'it is always there, come what may. It will be your shield in peace and war alike.' There is no need for the word to be framed with the lips, unless it is a help to do so, whether aloud or under the breath. The time will come when we can, as it were, mentally see the word where it lodges in the heart, and that is best of all.

But we should not feel bound to any word. A word is given for our help if we need it. The author writes (ch. 39), 'if God leads you to certain words, my advice is not to let them go, that is, if you are using words at all in your prayer.' Ultimately they will tend to slip away, and we shall be left simply looking into the heart and meaning God, and continuing to mean him and him alone. What the author insists on in regard to words, if they are used, is that they should be taken whole and not analysed. If, for example, we take the word 'God', we should resist the temptation to reflect on him, for this is not the time to consider discursively his love and goodness, nor his reconciling work in our Lord's passion. There is a time for that but it is not now; now is the time for knowing God and loving him, the time—inevitably we come back to the phrase—for 'reaching out with a naked intent of the will towards God', remembering always that, mentally, we should be looking into the heart and seeing him there.

The Cloud does not say much about posture. The author simply tells us that the body will of its own accord tend to take up the position most suited to prayer. In Chapter Sixty-one he writes,

> For when a soul is determined to engage in this work, then, at the same time, (and the contemplative does not notice it) his body, which perhaps before he began tended to stoop because this was easier, now through the Spirit holds itself upright, and follows physically what has been done spiritually. All very fitting!

Whether kneeling, sitting or standing, the back invariably tends to straighten out in this prayer, as all who practice it will know. We shall be returning to this question, but I would just mention here that older people, and perhaps many younger people too, may well find that sitting erect in an upright chair is the best position. There are some to whom sitting suggests a want of reverence, but we need hardly feel like that about a posture that our author may quite possibly have used himself. We know that it was the favourite posture of one of the great English mystics of the period of The Cloud. To quote from Father Verrier Elwyn's book Richard Rolle:

> 'Sitting', he would say, 'I am most at rest and my heart most upward. I have loved to sit, for thus I loved God more and I remained longer within the comfort of love than if I were walking or standing or kneeling.'

And we may recall that it was while the Church was seated that the Holy Spirit first descended upon it at Pentecost.

Described thus, prayer sounds easy enough, and indeed in Chapter

Three of *The Cloud* the author does make the claim that it is the easiest work of all, when a soul is helped by grace and has a conscious longing for prayer. No doubt there is a real sense in which that is true. We may recall the story of Jacob in the Old Testament, how he toiled seven years for Laban, in order to win Rachel's hand. From what we know of Laban, Jacob's work must have involved a good deal of sweat and tears, and yet, we are told, for the love that he bore to Rachel they seemed to him but a few days. It was love that made the work easy, and that is true also of our work of prayer. At the same time, the author is at no pains to conceal the cost involved. 'It is hard work', he writes, 'very hard work indeed' (ch. 26).

It is probably no accident that he refers to his prayer as work for prayer has about it two qualities which we normally associate also with work. On the one hand it is costly to the one who does it, and on the other, beneficial to the community, which includes the worker himself. If we are called to contemplative prayer and mean to respond to that call, we must face the fact that this will require a great deal of us—the sacrifice of time, courage to persevere, patience to endure the pain of deepening self-knowledge, fortitude in times of temptation, faith when the way is obscure, and the love which is ready to make every new surrender as the Spirit calls. That is one side of the work, the costly side, and we may well ask who is sufficient for these things? But there is too the other side, the social side which serves the community, and how can we serve the community better than by engaging in the work of healing and reconciliation, of making men whole within the Body of Christ? For that is the effective outcome of this work. It has been well said that contemplatives war against the real enemy, and ultimately against the only enemy, for whereas in the world we are up against effects, the contemplative is brought face to face with causes, with the ultimate truths which lie behind the visible.

★　　★　　★　　★　　★　　★

Some of my readers will remember a story by Robert Hugh Benson in which he tells of a lonely chapel where a nun is praying. To this chapel comes one whom we might call a visionary or a sensitive, someone who possesses unusually perceptive psychic sensibility. To the ordinary observer nothing is happening in that chapel— there is simply a nun praying—but to the visionary the unseen world discloses its secrets. Teilhard de Chardin re-tells the story:

> All at once he [the visionary] sees the whole world bound up and moving and organising itself around this out-of-the-way spot, in tune with the intensity and inflection of that puny, praying figure. The convent chapel becomes the axis about which the earth revolves. The contemplative sensitised and animated all things because she believed; and her faith was operative because her very pure soul placed her near to God.

'This piece of fiction', Teilhard adds, 'is an admirable parable', and he continues:

> If we could see the light invisible as we can see the clouds or lightning or rays of the sun, a pure soul would seem as active in this world by virtue of its sheer purity, as the snowy summits whose impassable peaks breathe in continually for us the roving power of the high atmosphere.

The author of *The Cloud* does not hesitate to make this sort of claim for his work on what we might call the community side. He writes thus:

> All saints and angels rejoice over it and hasten to help it on with all their might . . . Moreover the whole of mankind is wonderfully helped by what you are doing in ways you do not understand. Yes, the very souls in purgatory find their pain eased by virtue of your work . . . and in no better way can you be made clean or virtuous than by attending to this.

How little we know of our true helpers! Father Martin Thornton observes in *Christian Proficiency*:

> I rather feel that some of us are in for a shock when in the Church expectant we discover the real perspective for world redemption; the achievement of the Prime Minister and the Foreign Secretary may look pretty small compared with the influence wrought by little Miss Perkins of Honeysuckle Cottage.

And do we realise that as we grow older and the vigour of mind and body begin to decline, this is the work which the Holy Spirit desires to entrust increasingly to the faithful, the work which the author of *The Cloud* does not hesitate to describe as the most far-reaching and deepest work of all?

CHAPTER VII

Contemplation and the Cloud of Forgetting

OUR AUTHOR tells us us there are two clouds, not one, and it is to the second, the 'cloud of forgetting' that we must now turn our attention. We meet it first in Chapter Five where he writes as follows:

Just as this cloud of unknowing is as it were above you, between you and God, so you must also put a cloud of forgetting between you and all creation . . . Everything must be hidden under this cloud of forgetting . . . Indeed, if we may say so reverently, when we are engaged on this work it profits little or nothing to think even of God's kindness or worth, or of our Lady, or of the saints or angels, or of the joys of heaven . . . it may be good sometimes to think particularly about God's kindness and worth . . . yet in the work before us it must be put down and covered with the cloud of forgetting.

The author allows no exception. He goes on to specify everything that must be put under this cloud. We have already seen that any theological speculation is forbidden at this time; equally forbidden are all memories and imaginations of happy occasions and beautiful things, all the anxious thoughts and painful memories which may so often, even against our will, rise up and trouble us—memories of past sins long since repented and forgiven—all these are to be pressed down, like everything else, under the cloud of forgetting. This is not for the destruction of memory and imagination—at other times they will function in the ordinary way—but in and through the practice of this prayer they will be increasingly purified and we ourselves will grow in detachment from them. The near compulsive grip which memory and imagination may have upon us in certain areas of our lives will be broken, and as we give ourselves to this prayer the Spirit will lead us on into an ever growing freedom.

As the book goes on the author becomes yet more insistent on this cloud of forgetting. What is likely to cause special trouble, he says, is the memory of past sins, yet we are to be in no way disheartened by this. Here, in its entirety, is Chapter Thirty-one:

> When you have done all you can to make the proper amendment laid down by Holy Church, then get to work quick sharp. If memories of your past actions keep coming between you and God, or any new thought or sinful impulse, you are resolutely to step over them, because of your deep love for God; you must trample them down under foot. Try to cover them with the thick cloud of forgetting as though they had never been committed by you or anyone else. And indeed as often as they come up push them down. And if it is really hard work you can use every dodge, scheme and spiritual strategem you can find to put them away. These arts are better learnt from God by experience than from any human teacher.

Is there something alarming in the vigour of these words? Do they perhaps suggest 'repression' in the psychological usage of the word? By repression I do not mean the same thing as *suppression* of thought—something which occurs every time we choose to think of one thing rather than another as, for instance, when the bell goes, a schoolboy will suppress the thought of Latin in order to free his mind for mathematics. Repression as I am now using the word stands for a compulsory and involuntary forgetting of experience or memories which the mind has found too painful to retain in conscious thought. A mark of real repression is that the memory cannot be recalled at will, however hard the person may try. That does not mean it is out of harm's way—this is certainly no case of 'out of sight out of mind'—for it can send up all sorts of fears and compulsions to the conscious mind, and many people suffer physical disability—sickness, paralysis, blindness—through fears and conflicts which remain repressed. When I read somewhere, 'You mean, doctor, I have a boil in my unconscious?', it seemed to me a nicely graphic description of a repression. Psychologically speaking, *suppression* is harmless, *repression* is dangerous. It is convenient to have the two words, standing as they do for different concepts, and yet they cannot be kept entirely apart, for suppression could be followed by repression, if the former were persistent and the thought suppressed highly charged with emotion.

From what the author of *The Cloud* writes in the next chapter (Thirty-two) which we shall come to later, I think he would have been fully alert to the danger of repression, psychologically understood. The great spiritual directors were good psychologists, though since they lived in a bygone age their knowledge of the science was necessarily intuitive rather than analytical. I have been interested to read in Dr Morton Kelsey's book, *Healing and Christianity*, how he, the author, asked Jung what was the method of counselling nearest to Jung's own. He expected Jung to name one or other of the psychological schools, but instead he replied, 'The classical direction of conscience of the nineteenth century in France'. The directors of that period would have drawn freely on those before them; names such as St Francis de Sales, Fénelon, Caussade and others come to mind.

★　　★　　★　　★　　★　　★

Before we go further, let us distinguish between different types of memories. First there are what I shall call the emotionally neutral class, and these are by far the most numerous. What is it I have done today? Well, if I think back, I got out of bed, I washed and dressed, had break-fast, walked to work, and so on. All such memories belong to the emotionally neutral class, and if they recur during prayer they are not difficult to ignore and should cause no trouble. Then there are other thoughts which may be emotionally evocative, but in a pleasant and non-disturbing way. Such are the memories of beautiful scenery, great art or music, friendship and the like. These too are to be put down at the time of contemplative prayer, and it is unlikely that any problem will arise. More difficult to put away is the memory of some work in which the mind has been deeply engrossed, some business problem, some talk one is preparing, some difficult letter to be written.

However, in none of these cases is there a danger of repression in the sense in which we are using the word. But there are other thoughts which, for one reason or another, will fit into none of these classes, thoughts which are highly charged emotionally, due to some painful or traumatic experience, forgotten or largely forgotten, reaching back, perhaps, into early childhood; or to some persistent and it may be irrational fear which takes on the strength of a phobia we are virtually powerless to control. Morbid guilt, overwhelming grief, deep-seated resentment, wounded pride, jealousy, a sense of inferiority, scrupulosity, more or less compulsive aggressions—these are the kind of disorders, disguised as they may be in consciousness, which are likely to cause trouble. But we must take courage, for in our prayer they are finding their healing.

The author, as we have seen, has said that everything is to be pressed down under a cloud of forgetting, but, significantly, he immediately goes on to say how memories can be dealt with when they do arise, and here, as everywhere else, he is clearly speaking from his own experience. Let me clarify this seeming contradiction by a simple illustration.

Suppose you take your ten year-old son to church and, since he has a tiresome cough, you tell him not to cough during the sermon. At once you realise that this piece of advice standing alone will not do, yet it has value because it gives him something to aim at—without it he might cough freely and unnecessarily. 'But', you go on to say, 'if you must cough, try to cough into your handkerchief and then the noise will be muffled.' It is a very simple illustration but that is the sort of advice our author is giving. He is telling us not to let memories and imaginations invade our prayer, and this is valuable because it sets our sights on God alone, and on the word we have chosen to focus and hold our attention. Without that advice we should be lost from the start. However much this boy of ours may have to cough in church, it is essential he should get his priorities right and aim at self-control. If he doesn't he will spoil the sermon for everyone else and would have done better to stay at home. Equally, if we do not get our priorities right in prayer, if we do not firmly resolve 'to reach out with a naked intent of will towards God' so that mind and heart are occupied with nothing else but God himself, then we shall find ourselves given over to the memories and distractions which crowd in and our prayer time will be a disaster—daydreaming rather than praying—and it would have been better not to attempt it. But once our sights have been truly set on God, with the desire and intention that in God's grace they shall remain so, we need not fear these invaders of our imagination. What now becomes necessary is to pay them no attention. Later I hope to show that these very things are the means of our purification and healing, so long as we are content simply to let them be, and look over their shoulder, as it were, to God.

CHAPTER VIII

Contemplation and Healing

'LOOKING over their shoulder, as it were, to God'. With these words we have, in fact, anticipated the teaching of *The Cloud*; in Chapter Thirty-two we read:

> Do everything you can to act as if you did not know that these thoughts were strongly pushing in between you and God. Try to look over their shoulder seeking something else—which is God, shrouded in the cloud of unknowing.

We are then to keep looking towards God, to be ready to suffer distractions if need be, 'to let them float', in the language of popular psychology, but not to attend to them. We are neither to run away from them nor to encourage them, we are simply to look to God in the midst of them.

The word 'simply' is not meant to imply that this will be easy. It is not for nothing that the author calls prayer 'hard work', and there will be days when the going is tough. I am not suggesting a sinecure for retirement and old age! Rather, what I am describing will call for quite as much resolution in the realm of the spirit as climbing a mountain in that of the body—the work is for men, not for canaries. Here is a quotation from John Edward Southall, a Quaker of several generations ago, which describes an early experience of silence before God. A friend had suggested he should learn to be still in God's presence. This, he thought, would be an easy matter—but not at all. No sooner had he begun

> than a perfect pandemonium of voices reached my ears, a thousand clamouring notes from without and within, until I could hear nothing but their noise and din. Never before did there seem so many things to be done, to be said, to be thought, and in every direction I was pushed and pulled and greeted with noisy acclamations of unspeakable unrest. It seemed necessary for me to listen to some of them, but God said 'Be still and know that I am God'. As I listened and slowly learnt to obey and shut my ears to every sound, I found after a while that when the other voices ceased, or I ceased to hear them, there was a still small voice in the depths of my being that began to speak with an inexpressible tenderness, power and comfort.

This was an early venture into silence, made at a time when no doubt the writer's daily life was marked by all sorts of distracting and dissipating thoughts, and we may believe that as the spirit of recollection formed within him, this disturbance at the time of prayer tended to abate. But we must not over-simplify, for there will be disturbances in prayer whose origin is other than that of our lower consciousness. The gospels and the epistles both remind us of the forces of evil beyond ourselves. St Paul tells us that we fight not against flesh and blood, but against principalities and powers, against spiritual wickedness in high places. At such times too we may draw on fields of psychic force set up by other people far and near. Jung's postulate of a collective unconscious is suggestive here. However this may be, our own rule remains the same—to look to God, to mean God and to go on meaning God. In standing firm within the storm, accepting its batterings, yet looking beyond it to God himself, the end for which we and all men have been created, we are being used by the Spirit to neutralise and disinfect evil whatever its origin—and, more, to work for its transformation. This is the prayer-ward aspect of what St Paul says (Col. 1:24) about completing 'what is lacking in Christ's afflictions, for the sake of his body, that is the Church'.

We notice that John Edward Southall did not have just a single word such as 'God', or 'love', with which to focus his attention, but a complete phrase, 'Be still and know that I am God'. The author of *The Cloud* also commends this. In Chapter Seven he gives us this tenderly beautiful phrase in the power of which distraction may be overcome, 'Him I covet, Him I seek, and none but Him'. No doubt he would say here, as he has said of the single word, that we should take whatever sentence God gives us—from the Psalms, it may be.

Our author tells us that when the conflict is at its height, the image of looking over the shoulder to God, who is beyond, may need to be changed for another better suited to the challenge of prayer. We are, he says, to surrender ourselves to God in the hands of our enemies, and he bids us pay special heed to this suggestion 'for I think that if you try it out it will dissolve every opposition'. The picture might be that of a manacled prisoner, quite helpless and at the mercy of his conqueror, and all that is left for him to do is to give himself over utterly and completely into God's care. 'Why art thou so vexed, O my soul, and why art thou so disquieted within me?' When such words come spontaneously to our lips, that is the moment for complete surrender—not to our state or to our despondency—but to God in the midst of our state. That also was the psalmist's experience. 'O put thy trust in God, for I will yet give him thanks which is the help of my countenance and my God'.

★   ★   ★   ★   ★   ★

For an exposition of this trustful surrender, or 'abandonment' as it is more generally called, let us turn now to the classical spiritual writer on the subject, Père de Caussade, confessor and director in the eighteenth century to the Sisters of the Visitation in France. It will be good to draw briefly on his letters to these Sisters through which the theme of abandonment runs like a golden thread. To one of them he writes that when troublesome thoughts cannot be expelled from the mind—in this case he is speaking of excessive fears—'no other remedy remains but to bear this crucifixion in a spirit of total self-abandonment to the will of God'; and this is saying precisely what *The Cloud* is saying—'surrender yourself to God in the hands of your enemies'. We have of course at such times the perception—of faith, not of feeling, for 'clouds and darkness are round about us'—that God is holding on to us, never more perhaps than now. Imagine a cat holding her kitten in her mouth and making her way through the undergrowth. The journey may be a painful one for the kitten, leading through thorns and briars, but the small creature knows she is being held. That picture illustrates the passive side of the spiritual life; it needs to be balanced at other times by the active side and for that we need the picture of a baby monkey, who is not held, but clings for dear life to its mother as she makes great leaps from tree to tree. Just so is the Christian life a matter of holding on, until we are led into the knowledge that we are being held.

In all his many letters to the Sisters, Caussade never shows the least alarm at the afflictions they are called upon to bear. To another he writes, 'I will end this letter by telling you that your state is truly crucifying and for that reason sound, desirable, purifying and sanctifying.' He has already told her that the interior fever which seems to destroy her is indeed only destroying the impure and earthly elements, much as various poisons in the body are destroyed during the crisis of illness. This, he adds, is a sign of recovery, not of sickness. And of course he is right. Caussade is not talking here of the healing of the body but of the soul, or, if we prefer, the total healing of the whole man, and in modern language we should say, that in this standing in the storm, in patient endurance, with faith unbroken, the personality is being integrated, the disharmonies of our nature are being resolved into a single whole, we are being taken on by the Spirit to a fuller maturity in Christ, which in its turn makes possible a deeper relationship in love.

Naturally, this healing process is not restricted to the time of prayer. What is begun or comes into special prominence in our prayer life will be carried forward in all our occupations. For the man whose life is

D

immersed in the love and will of God in prayer, the healing will continue through the whole round of life—his work and recreation, his eating, drinking and sleeping, his family relationships, his service of others and their service of him. Further, we must see this healing process not just as something taking place within ourselves—the healing of all men is in some degree caught up in it. We cannot separate ourselves as though we were all little islands set here and there in a universal sea. We need an organic picture, such as St Paul gives us of the body, in which the healthy functioning of each part has its effect for good on the body as a whole.

Here then is our liberation, and in its measure it contains within it the liberation of all. I think of those undying words on the tombstone of Martin Luther King, 'Free at last, free at last, thank God Almighty, I am free at last!' Man longs for his full liberation, for liberation and the capacity for love go forward hand in hand. The opposite of liberty is bondage, and bondage means fear, and it is, as St John tells us, perfect love that casts out fear. That is to say, perfect love liberates, and we may therefore say that liberation makes possible the perfection of love. For purposes known only to God our liberation may often be delayed, finding its perfection only after passing through the gate of death and resurrection. We can only place ourselves in the hands of the Spirit, content to be taken on at his pace, believing that God's purposes are best served in ourselves, and through us in those around us, when we let him refashion us in his time and not in ours. Meanwhile our infirmities and oddities, our annoyances and quirks remain, serving not only to humble us, but perhaps to present the sort of challenge to those around us which each needs from the other, until at last we are brought, in St Paul's undying words, to 'the glorious liberty which belongs to the children of God'.

CHAPTER IX

Some Practical Points

TOGETHER we have studied *The Cloud* or, at least, what lies at the heart of its teaching, and we have learnt in some measure how we are to proceed in the prayer of contemplation, and how to deal with the memories and imaginations which threaten to defeat us. Let us now imagine that we are coming to the time of prayer.

But, first of all, why are we coming? Surely, because we believe in a general way that this is the kind of prayer to which the Holy Spirit is calling us. We have already discerned the signs of that call and we need not now refer to them again. But we are also coming because this *is*, for us, the time for prayer, the occasion of our self-offering. We are not coming because we feel like praying—perhaps we do, more probably we do not—and it may even be that praying is the last thing in the world we feel like doing. It is essential that we get this clear. To be ruled by feeling, by sense impression, is a mark of spiritual immaturity. The mature are ruled by faith. Every act of prayer is an act of faith. Father de Caussade wrote in *Abandonment to Divine Providence*, 'Faith is nothing else than a continual pursuit of God through everything that disguises, misrepresents, and so to speak annihilates him.' Is that not exactly what our feelings, our sense impressions—whether gathered from external events or from our internal vagaries—are continually doing? If Job, in that great drama of the Old Testament, deprived of his possessions, bereaved of his children, and afflicted with suffering, had relied on what he saw and heard and felt, he would have taken his wife's advice, cursed God and died. Only the eye of faith could penetrate the cloud of affliction experienced in the senses and affections and cry out, 'Though he slay me, yet will I trust him'. So too, when feelings are against us, whether before or during prayer, it is only by acts of faith that we can reject them for the frauds they are, and pursue our appointed way.

Nor need we complain because this is so—we ought rather to rejoice, for every temptation to deny prayer on account of feeling carries within it the opportunity to grow in faith. Archbishop Temple once said that if we prayed for patience, we must expect God to answer our prayer by giving us opportunities in which to exercise it. The same principle is true if we pray for faith or, for that matter, for any grace. This time of prayer is the moment when faith is nourished and quickened, and never more so than when mood and feeling are against us. Faith has been defined by C. S. Lewis as the activity of holding on to what reason has accepted, in spite of changing moods. It is, he says, telling mood and emotion where they get off when they threaten to carry out a blitz on the reason.

In the life of the spirit there has to be a stripping of the senses which involves throwing the whole burden on to faith, not because the senses are evil—no one who believes in the Incarnation can accept that—but because they are so supremely good that neither God nor man can be satisfied with anything less than the realisation of their full potential. And that can come about only through a cleansing process— the pruning of the vine that it may bear more fruit—a vital part of which takes place in the prayer that is informed by faith at those times when the senses are being deprived of what they are most wanting. As St John of the Cross tells us, man has to be led from the stage at which his will rests and feeds on sense experience, to one in which the joys of sense are not, ultimately, denied but known in liberty of spirit. That is the true joy for which we were created, and the experiences of aridity and the 'dark night' in prayer are a preparation for it, both by what the Spirit effects within us at the time and also by the creation (in the power of the same Spirit) of those dispositions which will enable us to meet the disciplines of life in such a way that he can use them to complete his work in us.

★　★　★　★　★　★

Yet there will undoubtedly be days when we shall need the support of a book to help us through the difficult seasons of prayer. We are like children learning to walk, and we need a rail to hold on to and to come back to after each unaided trial. It is better frankly to acknowledge and accept this need than to persevere in a way which may, for the present, be too hard for us.

Spiritual reading, as it is generally called, differs from discursive meditation in that the mind and imagination are now channelled very simply by the words or sentences before us. We do not think around our subject but accept each passage as it comes and allow it to 'dissolve in the mind as a sweet dissolves in the mouth'. The simile is Caussade's and could scarcely be bettered, as long as we remember that what the mind feeds on is always to descend to the heart. We read the passage slowly, extracting the flavour of each sentence before allowing ourselves to go on to the next. The successive pauses may last for a minute, or much longer, and even if whole periods of prayer sometimes pass in this way it need be no cause for worry. But as soon as we find that reading is coming in the way of a deeper silence, the book should be laid aside, at least for the time being. Until then our reading will give mind and imagination just as much material as they need on which to feed. This is no different in principle from the one word 'fixed firmly in the heart', or the single sentence recommended in *The Cloud*. Spiritual reading is performing the same function, but at an earlier stage, allowing the mind and imagination more diversity than can be supplied by the single word or sentence.

The passage needs to be chosen with care; anything which stimulates intellectual excitement or curiosity is worse than useless, and for that reason readings that are well-known are likely to be the most suitable— we shall not be so eager to see how the theme ends when we know already. We should let the Holy Spirit lead us to the books which will best minister to our varying needs. Psalms, hymns and some books of prayer lend themselves specially to being read sentence by sentence, with frequent pauses. Letters by masters of the spiritual life such as St Francis de Sales, Caussade, Fénelon and others allow for longer readings between each break, and the same is true of many spiritual classics, the *Confessions* of St Augustine, *The Imitation of Christ*, as well as other works both ancient and modern.

★   ★   ★   ★   ★   ★

Then, a second question in respect of our approach to prayer: how long are we here for? We shall certainly not get far unless we do fix a definite time—even if in practice it may often have to be cut short. How this is done will of course depend on circumstances, and those of a single person living alone will be very different from those of a busy housewife. But let us not overlook the possibility of keeping the prayer time in church where we shall be relatively free from noise and disturbance. Group meetings too, whether in church or elsewhere, can be a great help; we support one another in the silence, are encouraged to be regular, and the temptation to cut the time short is eliminated. Today the Holy Spirit seems to be calling many people in this way.

Then, thirdly, in what state have we come? Are we perhaps tense and keyed up? Certainly we do not come to prayer in order to be relaxed (though prayer will have this effect on us), but if we are tense it is doubtful if we shall ever have the resolution to begin. We need a 'phasing-in' period. In the East yoga is commonly used for this; taking up various postures helps to release tensions and lead the disciple into the stillness of meditation. Some people are now discovering this in the West (though I do not refer here to the schools of yoga which use it simply as a bodily discipline cut off from its spiritual roots). But there are other ways of phasing-in and we probably know how to find our own. For some people it will be gardening, for others knitting, weaving, music, going for a walk. What is common to all these activities, if they are wisely chosen, is that they help to relax body and mind.

Vocal prayer of the sort described earlier can also, of course, be a 'way in'— so can a very simple act of relaxation. Indeed to spend the first few minutes at the start of prayer in this way may often be the best way to begin. We hear a good deal about relaxation nowadays, and bearing in mind its close relationship with prayer, it will be worth saying a few words about it here.

First, what is *not* meant by relaxation is lazing away one's time in idleness. As a working definition I would suggest that a relaxed state is a state of creative awareness attained 'through the lessening and elimination of mis-directed tension and effort'. The quotation is from a brochure by Ursula Fleming, a teacher of relaxation (though I prefer to call her art 'creative relaxation') who goes on to describe it as a 'way of growth both in the life of prayer and into a fuller humanity'. The dictionary defines the word primarily in terms of loosening, slackening, reducing tension, but that is too negative for our purpose and whenever I use the word in the present context it should be taken to include also the positive idea of creative awareness.

Suppose we approach the subject from the point of view of human relationships. Have you ever said to yourself, 'I do enjoy spending an evening with X, I always come home so refreshed and relaxed'? Yet you did not visit X in order to become relaxed, but to get to know him better and take pleasure in his company and conversation—that you came away relaxed was a by-product of the event. And does it not, by analogy, ring true that if in our prayer we are really in touch with the creative love and being of God, we should emerge fresh and relaxed? But the illustration does not end there. On occasion you might equally have to say, 'My time with X yesterday was quite different from before—I was so tense when I arrived that I was unable to absorb what he was waiting to give me.' And you may well decide that the next time you visit him you will relax beforehand so as to be able to reap the full benefit of his company. Surely this too applies to prayer. We may be so tense before we begin that we can no more establish rapport with the Holy Spirit, nor he with us, than we could really meet our friend on that unfortunate evening. So if we feel tense before prayer, it makes sense to begin by relaxing in order to become more receptive to what the Spirit would give us. Prayer is not relaxation and relaxation is not prayer, but for the Christian a vital partnership exists between the two, and if, in the way of the Spirit's leading, you say that you are now going to relax for the love of God, you are proposing to do something at least as close to prayer as when you say you are going to garden for the love of God, or knit for the love of God. As we have already noted, all these and many similar occupations, by providing relaxation for mind and body, can help to lead us into true prayer.

Relaxation does not mean 'going all of a flop'—it does not mean doing nothing. It certainly may look to others as if you were doing nothing and you may on occasion think the same thing yourself. I sometimes say to people who think they are doing nothing in their prayer, Well, just for once, stop praying and *really* do nothing—make yourself a cup of tea, sink back into an arm-chair, let the mind go where it will. You will see how easy it is, and that will show you how hard you must have been working before. The same could be said about relaxation—even after a person has accepted the idea of it, the practice of relaxation will call for the same courage and resolution as the practice of prayer itself.

Yet we should proceed cautiously, and before we leave the subject it ought perhaps to be said that relaxation is not (as popular articles sometimes suggest) in itself a magic cure for all our troubles. The truth is that relaxation *per se* is neither good nor bad but morally neutral. In this respect it may be compared with sleep which has the same function of enabling us to perform our work more effectively, quite independent of any moral value attached to the activity of sleeping. Yet I suspect that relaxation (and sleep too), taken in its proper measure, has a built-in tendency towards goodness. However this may be, everything I am saying here is based on the presupposition that we are seeking a fuller knowledge of God and of his will and purpose in our lives—that is the context of our reflections. We are considering relaxation in relation to prayer, and prayer in relation to living. And we might remind ourselves that the kind of prayer we have been speaking of is allowed by the author of *The Cloud of Unknowing* only to those who are seeking to grow into the fullness of Christ and who believe they are being called to follow this way of contemplation.

★　★　★　★　★　★

Finally, we return to the question of posture in prayer. We pray as whole persons, not as disembodied spirits, nor yet as spirits inside a body as water is inside a bottle, but as a complex entity of body, soul and spirit. To neglect the role of the body would be to deny that side of our nature of which we are, generally speaking, most conscious. As we have already seen, if we want to go to sleep the sensible thing to do is to take up the posture best suited to sleep, and if we want to pray to take up the posture the body finds most natural for prayer. Like the author of *The Cloud* we may have already discovered that posture for ourselves.

The basic requirement in posture is that the back should be held straight in an easy tension. This applies in whatever position we adopt—whether we stand, sit or kneel upright; or kneel sitting on the heels, perhaps with the help of a cushion or a prayer stool. Sitting on the floor lotus fashion with legs crossed and feet tucked into the body is an inadvisable posture for most western people, unless they have trained themselves to hold it easily. The rule should be to adopt whatever position we can maintain without undue strain. Let us assume we have chosen to sit on an upright chair. Holding the back straight in an easy tension will assist a natural counter-relaxation of the temples and forehead, and the muscles of the face and jaw. The mouth should be shut, but not tightly so. The eyes will be closed, eyeballs down and relaxed, and we look mentally to the heart. The arms too will be relaxed, the hands resting relaxedly palms downwards on the upper part of the thighs, or palms upwards in the lap. The classic position for the head is erect, firmly set on the neck, the back, neck and head forming one straight line. Some find that when the head is slightly inclined forward it assists in looking mentally at the heart. You will notice how often we come back to the traditional Orthodox teaching of 'the mind in the heart'.

I believe there is value in knowing and saying these things but I would not wish to be over-assertive about them—I have great respect for the approach of *The Cloud*, which is to lay down no rules but simply allow the body to straighten out naturally to its correct position as the prayer proceeds. Yet I am sure there is need for this other approach as well and it must be left to the individual to find the right balance between the two.

Of course we are not going to imagine, that having adopted the most meticulously correct posture, we are now at prayer. All we have done is try to prepare for the Spirit to do his work in us. I have described only the dry bones of the valley, which the Spirit must breathe on and clothe with flesh if they are to live. Or again, we are like the servants at the wedding feast who were told to fill the water-pots with water. Only the Lord of life can turn it into wine.

CHAPTER X

The Practice of Contemplation

WE NOW COME to the prayer itself. Picture, if you will, three concentric circles. On the circumference of the outer circle are written the names of the five senses—*sight, hearing, touch, taste, smell*. Also written there are the words *imagination* and *memory*; and lastly, on the same circle, *intellect* and *will*. The space outside the circle represents the world of everyday affairs, and these nine faculties inscribed on the circumference are to be understood in their normal relationships to all the things which go on happening around us. As the Spirit enables us to pray we leave this outer circle behind and move to the circumference of the middle circle. And with us we shall take *memory* and *imagination* and also *intellect* and *will*, but not the five senses. These are left behind and so should be mentally erased from the outer circle, but only lightly, because we shall come back to them. It is easiest to understand what is meant by saying we leave the five senses behind if we think of it in relation to sight. In prayer we close the eyes and so shut out the visual sense altogether. We cannot in the same direct physical way shut out the other senses. For example, if a car passes on the road, we cannot escape hearing it, but as far as possible we pay it no attention.

Here we are then on the middle circle, and now we have to deal with memory and imagination. We can think of these as one, for memory is really part of imagination. When the imagination is aware of something which happened to us in the past we call it memory. When we simply imagine something outside our own experience, then that is pure imagination and memory plays no part. Only imagination, moreover, can have reference to the future. St John of the Cross likens these two faculties to a sixth sense, and it is not difficult to see why. I may close my eyes and shut out all that is visible, but I can still, in my imagination, 'see' my car in the parking place outside. There is even an English phrase for it, 'seeing with the mind's eye', which exactly expresses St John of the Cross's meaning. In the same way, if you are musical you can probably 'hear with the mind's ear', playing back to yourself through the imagination some favourite concerto. The same is true of all the senses and you will see at once where this line of thought is taking us. If it makes sense in prayer to close the eyes and cut out *seeing*, then it makes no sense at all to retain the faculty of 'seeing with the mind's eye'— that is to say, using imagination to recapture the sense of sight. It is pointless to bolt the doors of the senses against the thief and at the same time leave the windows of imagination and memory open. Either we leave the house open or we close it altogether. It will be clear that this argument applies equally to all the senses in their relation to memory and imagination.

My object in stressing this point is to reinforce the teaching of *The Cloud*. There, you will remember, we are told not only to look at the cloud of unknowing before us, but to put a cloud of forgetting beneath us. Memories and imaginations are to be resolutely stepped over or, to use another metaphor, we are to look over their shoulder to God who is beyond. And having just seen that memory and imagination are as it were a sixth sense— windows through which the thief may get into the house after we have locked all five doors—we are in a position to see why the teaching of *The Cloud* must be as it is, and could not indeed be otherwise. And that is a point gained, for while everyone accepts that it is quite reasonable to cut oneself off from sight, and as far as possible from noise and other distractions of sense during prayer, when it comes to the question of leaving behind memory and imagination as well, they ask whether perhaps this is not taking things a little too far. But we have seen that if we allow entry to these two faculties we might just as well allow it to the five senses, and that will be disastrous for our prayer.

But now we move in from this middle circle to the inmost circle, lightly erasing, for the time being, memory and imagination to which we shall return later. To the circumference of the third circle we bring *intellect* and *will*. 'Intellect' is now to be understood not in its discursive form but as the ability to know by intuition rather than reasoning, and 'will' is to be understood as the ability to love by a single act and not by a multiplicity of acts, as we normally do in everyday life.

★   ★   ★   ★   ★   ★

Here then the Holy Spirit has brought us to the heart of our prayer. In the language of *The Cloud* we are to lift up our hearts to God, with humble love to mean nothing but God, to try to forget all created things, to strike the thick black cloud of unknowing with the sharp dart of longing love, and on no account to think of giving up. The short word 'fixed firmly in the heart' as the focal point of our attention is to be 'our shield and spear'.

Yet we know only too well that memory and imagination, although left behind, will be continually trying to force their way in and divert our attention from this work of prayer. What are we to do then, when despite our desire to give our attention exclusively to God, we perceive these things trying to gain a foothold within us? Certainly there is nothing to be afraid of. If the will remains constant they can do us no harm or, more positively, they can become the means of strengthening the will in its resolution to mean God and him alone.

Here is a picture I have found helpful. Imagine you are taking a motor launch up a river and your eye is on the goal you want to reach—in this context, God himself. Coming downstream and floating by is all sorts of rubbish—bits of wood from broken-up packing cases, empty tins and bottles and soggy paper thrown overboard by picnic parties, flotsam and jetsam of every kind. All this represents the memories and distracting thoughts which float across the mind and seek admission during prayer. What are we to do with them? We are to let them float past us. *Floating*, as you probably know, is a word frequently used in practical psychology—let your anxieties float, we are told—and all this rubbish is to float. That does not mean we are to try not to see it. Even if we do so try it will not help; a part of the mind will inevitably be aware of it. The important thing is not to follow it, that is to say, not to occupy ourselves with examining the thoughts or fears or fancies which may at any moment present themselves. We are to let them come, see them briefly, and let them go. Zen Buddhism has a picture of distracting thoughts being like empty boats floating down a river, and bids us watch those boats but resist the temptation to jump on board.

Our position then with regard to this rubbish is that we neither encourage it nor do we run away from it. We notice it briefly and, without pausing to examine it, we pass on our way through it. It is in this experience of standing and looking to God that our healing is taking place. We have already seen in the last chapter that we cannot separate our own healing from that of others, that all mankind is in a measure caught up in what God is doing in us. And so this work of standing in the conflict is most truly a work of intercession, a work of reconciliation between God and all men, of whom I am one.

The world and the devil may have their part in this rubbish which is floating by, but much of it will be of the flesh—my flesh—using the word to stand for the whole lower nature: pride, anger, jealousy, along with avarice, gluttony lust and sloth. Memories float by, the unconscious may throw up material that the conscious mind had repressed and which now appears in disguise, just as dreams disguise the lower levels of the mind. Here is the carcase of a cat floating towards us—a pretty smelly piece of garbage this, and we shall get a whiff of it as it goes by—but never mind, it won't kill us. We have only to remain constant, looking to God our saviour and redeemer, as Peter, walking across the stormy water, looked to Jesus. It was only, we remember, when he ceased to look at Jesus that he began to sink. There will indeed be suffering in all this but it will be creative—the suffering of purgation and cleansing. The place where the Spirit is bringing our disintegrated personalities into unity and harmony is the place of healing. We may not know it at the time, but later we shall be able to say with Jacob, 'Surely the Lord is in this place and I knew it not'.

Illustrations tend to break down at one point or another and there is a weakness in the one we have chosen. We have said that we are to take our boat upstream with eyes fixed on the goal before us, which is God. This however gives us an image of 'God out there' which is not helpful for our purpose, when we have already stressed the importance of keeping the eyes of the mind directed towards the heart. So the limitations of our example must not mislead us here. You might also object that, so far, it suggests that only painful, disagreeable and worthless things will occupy the imagination during prayer, whereas we know this is by no means true. Not only rubbish, but swans and water-lilies, trees and clouds reflected in the stream will glide past our boat—in other words, memories of what is good and pleasing will also seek to claim our attention. Our rule here is as before. We may see but we may not examine. The point is that *all* considerations are as dross for our purpose at this time. To examine some memories selectively, 'when they are holy and promise well', would be to make us prisoners whose liberty is equally curtailed whether the rope that binds us is of silk or rough hemp.

Father de Caussade has another picture which may help us at such times. He says we are simply to allow these memories and distractions to drop away as one might let stones drop into the sea. We are to resist them by turning to God with renewed acts of trust and abandonment. We are ever to keep plunging ourselves afresh into the ocean of God's love. Fénelon calls this forgetting of self the most perfect penitence, 'because all conversion consists only in renouncing self to be engrossed in God'.

But we are not to be worried if our distractions do not drop away as we might wish. Sometimes these stones which are to fall into the sea appear to be more like rubber balls which float around us. What matters is that the attitude of our will should be like an open hand, ready to let go. The very act of opening the hand helps us to let go with the mind. We may encourage ourselves with an old Chinese proverb, 'You cannot prevent birds flying round your head, but you can prevent them making nests in your hair.'

★　　★　　★　　★　　★　　★

And now our prayer time is over. What is it we have been doing? Well, in a sense, we have been taking a holiday, and if that sounds an odd way of putting it, remember that holidays often include doing hard and challenging things, like climbing mountains, or exploring unknown country. But this has been the best sort of holiday, for not only have we 'got away from it all'—which is essential on any holiday—but we have been in touch with the fount of all life and so have found re-creation of mind, body and spirit. We know how important it is to get away from our work from time to time, not to neglect it, but in order to see it in the perspective of eternity. And so we return to our work as before, and yet, not quite as before, for in this prayer the Holy Spirit has been active in the depths of our being, cleansing and purging us, healing and unifying the various sides of our nature. As a result we bring to our work a deeper integrity, a clearer perception of the real needs of those around us and—having come to grips with these things within ourselves—a fuller understanding of the fears and tensions which threaten to overwhelm others. Above all we bring a love disciplined and made strong through an ever deeper union with God himself.

EPILOGUE

'Love is my meaning'. These words, adapted from Mother Julian, hold the key to all that has been said and all that can still be said, whatever the nature of our calling in prayer. No method of prayer can of itself be valid apart from the dimension of love. In prayer love is expressed and deepened, and yet more, it is re-fashioned as, in an ever renewed dying and rising again, it takes its form from the wisdom and perfection of God. The saints are the great lovers, but it is God's love which is shed abroad in their hearts, and no other than God's redeeming and saving love will avail. 'At eventide they will examine you in love.' So wrote St John of the Cross, and the quotation is commonly ended there. We need to reflect that he at once went on to say that it is not the human love of our natural temperament of which he speaks, but the love which partakes of the nature of God's own love. And this he describes elsewhere as a living flame which tenderly wounds the soul at its deepest centre. What a corrective is this to our own poor human notions, often more sentimental than strong, more possessive than pure, more spoiling than wise, more tolerant than true! How well would St John of the Cross have understood—and we too shall grow to understand—the saying which an early tradition attributed to Jesus, 'He that is near me is near the fire'!